LOVE And HEALING

Without Knowing

God Was

Really There

VOL. 5

Love

And

Healing

Without Knowing

God Was

Really There

VOL. 5

with

OSCAR DIXON

© Copyright 2019 by Oscar Dixon,r

PRAYERS by FIRST EDITION: SCRIPTURES AND COMMENTARIES:

New International Version King James Version Strong Exhaustive Concordance Word Study New Statement Word Study Dictionary Thayer's Greek

All rights reserved. No parts of this book may be reproduced in any form without permission in writing from the publisher, writer, and editor.

All rights reserved. No parts of this book may be reproduced in any form without permission in writing from the publisher, writer, and editor.

No part of this publication may be reproduced, stored in a retrial system, or transmitted in any form or by any means or electronics, mechanical, photo-copy, recording, or otherwise without prior consent or permission focus on the family.

ISBN: 978-1-943409-65-5

All Rights Reserved

Table of Contents

DEDICATION 8
Love and Healing 11
Chapter One 13
Chapter Two 20
Chapter Three 27
Chapter Four 32
Chapter Five 40
Chapter Six 46
Chapter Seven 53
Chapter Eight 60
Chapter Nine 66
Chapter Ten 71
Chapter Eleven 77
Chapter Twelve 82
Chapter Thirteen 87
Chapter Fourteen 93
Chapter Fifteen 100
Chapter Sixteen 108
Chapter Seventeen 115
Chapter Eighteen 122
Chapter Nineteen 128
Chapter Twenty One 140
Chapter Twenty Two 146
Chapter Twenty Three 153

Chapter Twenty Four 158
Chapter Twenty Five 165
Chapter Twenty Six 171

DEDICATION

Rev. Frank D. Dixon Mrs. Ethel M. Dixon

During my youth, I don't remember home life with an uncomfortable lifestyle; our parents had a harmonious relationship. I don't remember loud boisterous voices and disagreements coming through the house in the midst of seven children.

My innocence betrayed me as I grew older. What I was experiencing was not the norm in other homes; we had hard times, shortages of everything, but the love of our parents for us and the Lord, words can't describe.

My dad and mother were always hugging and playing with us. I didn't know it then, but there were spiritual blessings of impartation placed on our lives. We grew up; passing on to our children what we received from our parents; the Lord of their lives, is the Lord of our lives. We believe the Lord brought our parents up the rough side of the mountain and set them on a solid foundation in Christ Jesus the Solid Rock; and so it is with us. I also dedicate these writings and testimonies to our parents, sisters and brothers; to tell the story is to be in concert with our upbringing.

Love and Healing

Vol. 5

Chapter One

JUST CALL HIS NAME

I Peter 2:24 (niv) He himself bore our sins in His body on the tree, so that we might die to sin and live for righteousness; by his wounds you have been healed.

It is taught and preached often that the Holy Spirit will give us a message in our dreams or visions. It may be for now or a time in the future. I received this scripture, Revelation 13:17 in my vision and it concerns the number of the beast and its mark. Our times have become difficult and truth is according to who is speaking at the time. We have the word of the Lord to speak truth to power. We can gather truth from our Bible studies and a good Bible-based church (there aren't as many as we would like to think.) An established Bible-based church and our studies will help us understand how to stand on the word of the Lord and avoids traps and potholes that lead to bad choices. I've gotten back to "just call his name."

I was disturbed about the information I had received in my vision. I continued to pray for revelation knowledge and a deeper understanding on what I had received. Late that morning the television was on and a woman was telling her story about the many difficulties she suffered in her life. There was a time she considered hurting herself. She remembered asking the Lord for help and immediately she began to feel a calmness and a belief came over her that the Lord had come to see about her in a desperate time in her life. What the Lord did for her, he'll do same for anyone who would "just call his name."

I believe this was my answer. The Lord new I hadn't been doing well. I've called His name so many times. He then sends a testimony to inform me all is well. While the testimony is going on, I'll feel a very warm presence; I believe it is the Holy Spirit. That's my confirmation that I'm going to be all right; I can trust His covering.

A few days later I was raising my voice at my grandson because his school work wasn't up to par and he was also leaving dinner plates on the table. He is my little rascal because I sit in his school room classes with him until he learns how to harness that beautiful energy. This little guy is reading a book in class while the teacher is giving out instructions for the new mathematics. I would give him a strong look, he would put the book away but by then the teacher had finish explaining how to solve the problems. I said, this guy hadn't heard too much of what the teacher had been saying while reading his book. The teacher passed out the test of about four questions, then she said turn your papers over and you have ten minutes to complete. This little rascal turns his paper over and finishes third on this test, without giving much attention to the teacher's instructions.

I'll remind each of us, be careful how we talk and discipline our children, grandchildren, and others. Often we forget who is listening to all we say and do. The Lord knows all things; we must line up with His Word. Grandson was at my home and his grandmother was trying to help him complete his homework. I came into the room and raised my voice, "listen to your grandmother, finish your homework". I was walking away and I heard in my spirit, "I have the same problem with your disobedience." I realize the Lord is creator; He looks at our behavior, habits and attitudes and judges whether they are good or displayed badly. I am trying to be more like Christ.

After this encounter and other encounters, I began to look and listen very carefully at my words, attitudes and actions toward him and others. Hearing the voice of the Lord in my spirit was powerful and it frightened my very existence. It is a priority to talk with consideration to everyone no matter the situation. I always have been kind and respectful to everyone and we always grow from our experiences. Whatever I am, the Lord wants me to improve. He says, "I want you to take on the mind of Christ."

A few days later, I was going over in my mind those very words from our Lord. To my surprise I felt his presence a while back when the Lord brought this remembrance to me as well. In this warm presence I heard in my spirit and the statement struck a chord of fear in me. I heard, "He will be closer to me than Ruth to Naomi." I have read the book of Ruth and that relationship represents great love, respect, devotion, with a mind made up, "where you go, I'll will go". The Lord is telling me He is establishing a relationship, a bond between Him and I. This is a dream come true, it is frightening but is also rewarding to have a covenant with the Lord.

TRANSLATION: I Peter 2:24 (niv)

Christ died for my sins, in our place, so we would not have to suffer the punishment we deserve. Jesus Christ became our substitute for our atonement. He died on the cross, so that we can be finished with sin and live a good life from now on for his wounds have healed ours.

Chapter Two

HE SENDS MESSAGES

John 15:7 (niv) If you remain in me and my words remain in you, ask whatever you wish, and it will be given you.

Thursday morning my upper tooth and gum began to bother me and it did again that evening. The discomfort bothered me a great deal during my classes at the institute. I had even purchased toothache cream to help reduce the discomfort. I put my mouth guard in that night and was surprised that the pain began to cease immediately. The next morning and during the night it started aching again. A thought came to my mind, call your dentist office to see if you could get and emergency walk in.

I talked with the receptionist and she gave me a walk-in time of 11:00 am; this was more than I could hope for. I arrived and went directly into a dentist chair and the tech came in and took x-rays of the upper gum. A few minutes later, the dentist came in and examined me and found no damage or missing fillings or damaged caps. She supposed something caused me to bite down very hard on occasions which may have caused the discomfort. I told her some of the information concerning family issues. She thought something could have triggered that nerve and created the discomfort, but not likely.

I explained, that I had lost some energy. Since then I have visited a health institute to catch up on my organic green juices, wheatgrass juices and salads to get my energy levels back up. My dentist became interested in who worked with me, so I dropped a name. She smiled as she identified with the person's name and the company; both of them she was very familiar with.

My dentist informed me a friend stopped by the other day and brought her fresh green drink and it was very good. I began to have this warming presence, this fulfilling I get from the Holy Spirit. His presence brings on the tears as I sat in the dentist chair. He says, "tell her to start juicing," I told her, she said, "I received it". She looked at me a little strange and concerned that he could speak a word and I felt it in my spirit. I explained to her, I have and anointing of a prophet on my life, "which would help explain those pleasant trips I take into the red clover field when I meditate while you are doing your dental work on me. I go into meditation to hear from our Lord and Savior, the Christ."

For those who don't know about red clover, I grew on the farm where the property owner plants acres of red clover for the milk cows. My task as a sharecropper's son was to send the milk cows into the clover fields for a short period of time and allow them to eat the red clover. This made the milk more nutritional and the production was greater. If you check your vitamin shops today, you will find red clover blossom and other forms of it and the nutritional value is good for you.

I explained that, "when the Lord really loves us, He sometimes sends a witness to make sure you receive his word with understanding." I said, "as a matter of fact, I was the second word" and I explained that the Holy Spirit always sends a word at least two times. "Your friend suggested juicing, I am suggesting the same. Because I heard this in my spirit this is the second word". She said she never knew that.

I said in my thought, Lord, you didn't bring me all the way down here to tell her that. I believe I heard in my spirit, "yes." The presence of the Holy Spirit was very strong and He filled me with tears. The Holy Spirit's presence moved me to pray for her and to bless her health and her hands. My dentist supposed, if that was true my tooth situation may very well be to inform her and she didn't find a tooth problem. She thanked me and didn't bill my account for the examination and the x-rays. We discussed methods of juicing. She seemed very receptive. Juicing your greens often aids in preventing health issues. Juicing helps purify the blood and puts more oxygen into the blood stream. Trust the Lord for your health and well-being. Remember He is the Lord of your life who answers prayers, especially for those who trust in Him.

TRANSLATION: JOHN 5:7 (niv)

Most of us try to be good and those of us who believe they are honest do what is right; Jesus Christ tells us the only way to live a truly good life is to stay close to Him, like a branch attached to the vine. If we try to operate aside from Him, our efforts are unfruitful. Christ is our Vine, we are His branches, we will abide in Him and received the full nourishment that life offers us through Christ.

Chapter Three

From My Stick to God's Staff II

Psalms 34:9 (niv) Fear the Lord you saints, for those who fear him lack nothing.

This walking stick for me came into being when I lived in New York. I would walk up in the woods and I felt it necessary to have help in the event I encountered an activity that is greater than I. For me this is leverage and supports me when the scales are tilted against me.

There were many occasions as a paper boy in Tuskegee when the dogs waited patiently for me every morning to ride by with papers for those houses. I rode up the long hill with papers, our bikes in those days didn't have gears. When I walked my bike, the dogs wouldn't bother me. When I put foot to the peddle, they were after me like a bad habit, barking and biting at my heels until I got my speed up and my Schwinn bicycle carried me to victory, seven days a week I met the challenge.

I had two methods of transportation to cover my news paper route, my Schwinn bicycle and my mule, Lou. The terrain to deliver my papers was hazardous especially for my bicycle and it gave me bent rims. There were no problems with the barking and biting with my mule, Lou, who seemed to always have an attitude. If the dogs came close, she would kick them. When I got off her to deliver a paper and didn't tie her, she would walk all the way home and not get in the street. Needless to say, Lou left me with a stack of papers still to be delivered.

Growing up on the farm, it was normal to walk with a walking stick. Traveling through the woods we often encountered an enemy; the stick was our angel, our protector while the Lord was always watching over Rev. Frank's children. There was this particular occasion, many years later in my home getting ready for retirement. We had gotten heavy snow that night. Late the next day I was walking in the nearby woods beyond my home on the private camp property of about 30 acres that wintry afternoon. It was a beautiful sunny day after the snow had fallen. I couldn't resist going for a walk, crushing along on the snow.

What I enjoyed the most about walking, the sun was beaming down and glancing off the white driven snow; it was simply beautiful and warm. Today I can truthfully say only the Lord manifests such beauty.

This particular day I was walking and I had gone a good distance from home. Looking to my left going Northward there was this much feared dog, a pit-bull of all animals, what a big guy. He saw me before I saw him. He had cut me off from my house since I was walking far out on the 30-acre property. Once I saw him, his reputation preceded him. There was no effort made to let him know I had seen him and I started scanning for a weapon to meet the challenge. I was running out of real estate, I was surveying for another house or sticks and to my surprise a downed tree, partially in the snow. It was off to my right; the pit bull had the left side cut off.

I went over to the tree buried in the show and pulled on a large limb and it broke free. It was a big limb but wasn't strong enough to engage big guy. I took the big limb for my walking stick and headed back towards my home raising my Moses Stick up and down. I looked over my right shoulder, big guy realized I had support and I don't mean with that rotten stick. I believe the Lord showed him several angels surrounding me as I returned home. Big Guy was dropping further and further back then he stopped. I would venture to say big guy said, I can take the one guy but God, there is to many of the others, they don't look like they are from my neighborhood.

TRANSLATION: Psalms 34:9 (niv)

You say you belong to the Lord, but do you fear him? To fear the Lord means to show deep respect and honor to him. We demonstrate true reverence by our humble attitude and genuine worship. No matter what it looks like, we must learn to trust the Lord for all things, there are no overnight wonders, to seek our Lord to cover us and know He is with us is to learn to trust Him and be obedient to His word.

Chapter Four

A DESIRE TO RELEASE PAST HURTS

Psalm 25:7 (niv) Remember not the sins of my youth and my rebellious ways: according to your love remember me, for you are good, O Lord.

There has been a young man that had been working for a couple of my friends who have a transportation service. They hired this young man and trained him how to clean and detail the vehicles professionally.

He observed very closely the quality of their work and he was obligated and expected to maintain this level of service as well. You can imagine the training and follow-up was continuous until the day they inspected the equipment and initialed it satisfactory. Getting the work to this level called for work ethics to be demonstrated. The young man must show a desire to demonstrate he has the energy, the attitude and the integrity to take the assignment and know his work will go beyond the work shop. The customer will have the last word, and when they speak the company listens.

The relationship didn't go very well with the young man. He seemed unwilling to put his best foot forward. However, we continued to work with him and when his issues and attitude became personal and handicapped his reliability, there were necessary steps to be taken. There was a need to work with him through his situations and give him the support he needed to realize a desire to release past hurts. I took personal time with this young man to explain that I have experienced these dangerous times in my young and older life.

Fortunately for me, my dad and mother and older siblings had a structure of accountability for us to follow. When one of us strayed left too long, another sibling would check you. If we didn't yield promptly, that family member would bring in more heavy artillery. This would bring in our two oldest siblings to get us grounded. If that wasn't high enough up the power chain, they would drop a quarter; a long-distance call back home to mother, Ethel Mae or dad, Rev. Frank. Whoever was out of line, they didn't want to hear from back home. Let's be clear, there weren't any threats made. We know Ethel Mae who walks with the "Most High" and Rev. Frank as well would send a word that frightened you out of your sleep. Mother or dad in most situations would send a word to the oldest sibling and she would carry it out. Plus she was known to add to the prescription.

Dad's powerful words from "On High," would say, if you don't straighten yourself out; "I'll tell the Lord about you." I remembered one occasion, the storyline said, the older male sibling had been warned that his habits were unbecoming, out of line, and disobedient and he'd better straighten himself out.

At this junction in his life and life style, I am not certain which was more powerful, the word he had received from home or the action that took place one night which was the surprise of his life. I am not saying the word from home failed. I may be suggesting our Lord and Savior has a sense of humor and that He put His Word and actions together to achieve a more beneficial result. Late one evening the sibling was at his hangout, sharing laughter and good fun for the evening.

When the evening lost its laughter, our sibling was bent over the pool table for his next shot. Because of the interruption that just took place the noise ceased, he looks up into our oldest sibling's face and before he could explain, she was dishing out some almost unintelligible instructions on what could happen to him right then. From what little I know, he didn't walk that way anymore; it was far safer to follow instructions.

Family, our take away in this particular episode touches base on what accountability looks and feels like. This action was in house and over the years, there were many occasions when a family member took notice of family members and friends who were walking in the wrong direction, by joining the wrong crowd. They were talked with and were given understanding of what right feels like and to share their change with others.

This is a hard task, transforming the mind and reforming of our ways to follow the Lord. The Lord has given the believers a mandate; to extend our efforts to save those who are lost. We must be diligent in establishing a line of communication to save our young folks and the old ones who know better but haven't turned to our Lord and His saving grace. I am very aware of the trap that has been set for our young and old. The traps are used to help fill the prisons and to meet incarceration numbers for those who own these prisons.

I know the Holy Spirit is leading and guiding me in this journal. (In this paragraph The Holy Spirit speaks very strongly). The face that I saw in my vision was pleasant, but seemed distant, unhappy, with despair and a deep longing for something with uncertainty of what it is. We need the transforming order of the Lord.

This look hasn't escaped me, over the years it reminds me that I have seen this look of hopelessness and despair on so many faces of our youth and older men and women; but more specifically, our young men. I pray the Lord will send more laborers, for the harvest is plenteous.

TRANSLSATION: PSALMS 25:7 (niv)

This plea we must rely upon, feeling our own unworthiness, and satisfied of the riches of God's mercy and grace. How boundless is that mercy which covers forever the sins and follies a youth spent without God and without hope! Blessed be the Lord, the blood of the great Sacrifice can wash away every stain.

Chapter Five

WHAT DOES GOD EXPECT FROM ME?

> James 2:24 (niv) You see that a person is justified by what he does and not by faith alone.

If this question had been asked of me a few years ago my answer would have been quite different than what it is today. I thought a few years ago that I was a decent person, fair as possible, respectful to others, even to those who weren't so kind to me. I wouldn't allow that to disturb my peace. I learned to avoid uncomfortable situations and I have always been helpful to whomever I could. Our parents taught us to share with others at every opportunity that presents itself. Am I a child of the Highest God?

I even took the Lord's credit for things He blessed me to do. Even in my youth I came up with excellent ideas on how to do jobs and all through the years I had this unique ability to learn new methods and techniques to get work done. Out of my ignorance I would say "that's an Oscar"; this started in my early years. Just like other children we called it bragging about who could do this and who could do that. Of course, my learning and understanding was naïve. My terminology never occurred to me I should be praising the Lord and that all the blessings we have comes from our Lord and Savior, the one who is "The Gift Giver of Life." I have served in the church as a volunteer and

I serve on several boards. I always gave my gifts, my offerings and my tithes and did repair jobs throughout the church and property. As I grew in my spiritual life, there seemed to be more attacks coming on me in the least expected ways especially on my job.

My prayers became increasingly longer, and more often I was seeking answers and understanding for the things that I was hearing because the work I was doing was far beyond my knowledge and understanding.

When someone would complement me on my strategies with the labor board and ideas that became a powerful financial savings for the company, I made this comment "that's and Oscar." I knew this was not of me, only the Lord could give out that kind of word that was precise and that bridged the company and union to accept my suggestions to end a job slow down and a possible job strike. I knew God was the giver and doer of all the successes that I was experiencing. I became more knowledgeable of the word and realized, even at my young age at the time, I was responsible to learn to praise the Lord for the mind and the ability to do jobs beyond any training are experiences I had acquired. I decided, I would give God all his glory, praise and thanks.

I began to get convicted in my scriptures and when ministers were preaching. I realized that I had better find out what the Lord is saying to me. Through scriptures, prayer, patience, and fasting, the Lord began to direct me.

When I said to the Lord that I would serve him, the Lord began to reveal to me that I was his creation and there was a planned purpose for my life from the beginning. In the past, what I was doing hadn't scratched the surface for what He had purposed for my life. To have works is a good thing as the book of James clearly states. When I became a servant of the Lord my seeking began to be revealed that we are chosen to an everlasting work. Becoming Christlike is part of His plan in perfecting us with His character in serving the Lord of our lives.

TRANSLATION: James 2:24 (niv)

We are not justified by what we do, not in any way. True faith always results in deeds, but do not justify us. Faith brings us salvation; active obedience demonstrates that our faith is genuine.

Chapter Six

A PLAN MISSION

Matthew 9:37 (niv) Then he said to his disciples, "The harvest is plentiful, but the workers are few.

Our ministers and leaders are birthing a mission field out of The Community Church. For me this speaks volumes for those who would love to participate by giving of themselves, their time and their resources.

The impact will go forth into the community and care for the need of others. This sacrifice of love, labor, and personal resources demonstrates the desire to go into the community and grow their faith by what they experience through the mission team. The healing begins any time others step out on faith in the form of a mission team. This touches the very heart of the Lord. The ministers and the leaders have prayed for and received doctors, nurses, aids, intercessors, and evangelists. We have become that "awakening spirit" in the communities and it can perform at home and abroad with power and authority from on High. The Lord loves discipleship as he says, "save my lost sheep bring them back to the fold." "Remember, I purpose these gifts in you from the beginning, go yonder in to all nations preaching the gospel, teaching and healing and bring my children back into the fold."

I believe our Most High God, touched His Son and said, look what is happening in the Community Church, with strong leadership, they have gathered themselves a team of disciples that will fill the void for so many. Christ, I believe, agreed with his Father and said we will watch over their works and everywhere their feet tread we will bless them and place and anointing on each of their lives. When they call upon my name, I will answer, speedily. Family, as I recorded this in my journal, I was moved deeply by His presence. The Christ will always be with those who do His work, it's generational. Good seed is nourished and watered by the Lord to continue to bring forth fresh fruit from on high. Thank you, Lord, for birthing us with your love, protection and provisions. It is true you are our Jehovah Jireh our provider.

The Community Church is already established as the model through sound leadership. It has already sown seeds that are yielding an excellent harvest. I remember hearing upon our arrival with The Mission Team, the people walked great distances to be in place for the medical team, because their needs were so great. Each time we have gone there, we expanded our base of operation and gave the best of ourselves. I believe we touched the heart of God and He is very pleased. We can sow new seeds in a community-based mission that is organized out of a local body. We united the people and went abroad equipped in spirit, supplies and volunteers to fill the necessary positions that will treat our children and the women. We can do good in this place as we give others the opportunity to join the mission field working and gaining experience.

Many of our church family need to have that

experience; getting involved in making a difference, helping to reshape people lives and giving them hope. While reshaping other's lives, those of us who are involved we will be reshaped as well. We will have that desire to take our experiences in the mission field abroad. In the planning stages, there will be a strategy that sets a criterion on what area and community and set the guidelines for our youth. Our youth are our trainees for mission fields that will go abroad in the future. Our youth and adults will receive training on what to expect and how to respond when these conditions are before us. As part of our plan, I would like to see different levels of exposure for our teams who will be involved in preparing for the mission trip. We would want them knowledgeable on every aspect of how the mission trip unfolds.

I would suggest we establish in our mission field, what I call "The Not Forgotten Ones."

These are former members that we can set a criterion for them and plan what we can do to enhance their lives and let them know that we love them and haven't forgotten them. We will establish the need and follow through with a day of cutting hedges, raking leaves or going inside with a prepared meal and breaking bread with our family's members in their varied community. Our leaders have experienced this with others and the response and appreciation was deeply felt. This effort establishes our connection with the community and it will grow from inside out with our youth and adults fortified with the experiences from mission teams who have left large foot prints for others to follow.

TRANSLATION: Matthew 9:37 (niv)

Jesus looked at the crowds following him and referred to them as a field ripe for harvest. Many people are ready to give their lives to Christ if someone would show them how. Jesus commands us to pray that people will respond to this need for workers. Often when we pray for something, God answers our prayers by using us. Be prepared for God to use you to show another person the way to Him.

Chapter Seven

THE BATTLE ISN'T YOURS

II Chronicles 20:15 (kjv) And he said, hearken ye, all Judah, and ye inhabitants of Jerusalem, and thou king Jehoshaphat, thus saithe the Lord unto you, be not afraid nor dismayed by reason of the multitude; for the battle is not yours, but God.

Tonight, I opened my e-mails, like any other night and to my surprise I received this e-mail that says, "who are you?" This happened to be a class group on this listing. I didn't join the group, someone added my name and I began receiving e-mails from classmates. Observing closer, I wondered who on this group would ask this question, "who are you?" With no way to tell, I e-mailed back my name and asked who wants to know. The wire was still hot when I received a return with their name; we were classmates. A few days later, I received a call from this long-ago classmate. They were elated and remembered me. In the old days I was paper boy and cut lawn for my pennies to keep soles on my shoes. We talked and a new relationship was established. Thank you, Lord.

This former classmate asked me to be a praying friend for her. There are issues happening in her family and prayer support would be great to have. While listing to her personal story, I was moved to keep her in prayer. I remember such a time in my youth, "the Journey Begin," when I needed a friend that understood me when dad's conference relocated him and I had a new school to begin in. I was shame faced and felt lost. One day my teacher called me to her desk, handed me a note and sent me on and errand. That was a divine move from the Lord. That one occasion led to personal time working with me and many occasions as the years passed. My teacher introduced me to reading and acting in school plays. I always was a lead person, which means I had to learn a great deal of material.

I believe Mom and Dad were somewhere in the night and day wearing out their knees, saying, "Oh Lord, when will this boy hold up his head and allow people to talk with him." Lord, Ethel and I are doing all we can to open him up. Lord, fix his life so he can hold up his head and not be a shamed. Lord we need a great farm season this year, the children are getting older and they eat more, with the crop you give us they will work harder as well."

"The Battle Is Yours Lord, we thank you now for all you're doing for us." Family, you guessed correctly, the lights came on. I realized I could learn the lines and remember what I read and studied. Acting in plays began to remove the shame from my future and I was encouraged. I don't know if my teacher realized the pain she removed from my life. When I visited her over the years, I would stop by her home and thank her for teaching me to believe in myself. The kindness shown me gave me confidence. I haven't stop extending my hand to others.

After all the years have passed, we are still communicating. I had prayer with her desiring that the Lord meet her family's needs. It is important to share and be a blessing. I remember my down times and more than the occasions I can count, the Lord has always sent help by His powerful hand.

I was moved to send words of Love and Blessings in this book, to let you read what the Lord is saying to us. It reads; I don't know why I am quoting this, "Let not your heart be trouble," I received in the spirit, we have the Holy Spirit waiting with open arms for you to give Him your troubles. I know you know the scriptures and are a prayer warrior of faith. When there is disagreement in the family, only the Lord knows the heart on each of us and what is our real situation. Knowing this, give your problems over to the Lord and leave it with Him, you must learn to trust Him.

As I wrote this, I felt the presence of the Holy Spirit, so know that He is in this with you already. As I finish the note to you, I will declare the love of God on your life and don't try and fix stuff that is bigger than you are. Stay in prayer and know you are covered in the love of the Holy Spirit. Call me when you think of my name, often the Lord does that, you didn't accidentally, gently think of me, the Lord is speaking to you. There is blessing in obedience, I ask you to hear His voice and trust in the Lord.

TRANSLATION: II Chronicles 20:15 (kjv)

The Lord spoke; don't be afraid or discouraged, the battle belongs to the Lord. Every day we fight temptation, pressures and the unknown of this dark world. Their task is to try and get us to rebel against God. We are spiritual beings of God, we can ask for help in our struggles and God will fight for us. God always triumphs, he does not have limitation as man does. God strength can work through our fears and weaknesses that we work for him and are led by the Spirit of God.

Chapter Eight

God Will Provide Lift-

Mark 3:35 (niv) Who ever does God's will is my brother and my sister and mother.

Most of this year, my project was to remove many of the trees that are very tall and dangerous that can reach my house, garage or vehicles in the event of a bad wind storm. I planned to make good use of the oak trees in particular, they make great fire wood. The trees are sawed up, the wood is busted up and stacked.

After a few months, the wood has cured and I am ready to load my truck and deliver some to my friend and family down in Alabama. When I built the two houses south of where I am, it was in my spirit to add a fireplace and a pot belly stove. With foresight and good intention, it was done. A few years later hard times did come and the family made great use of the stove, fireplace and firewood.

The dump truck was loaded, and my very good family friend volunteered to deliver the first load to our prayer team deacon. Early that morning the load was end-route, regardless of the good intention to provide a blessing for others, the best prepared plans don't always work out. I am thankful that I invited the Lord into my efforts and asked his blessing, traveling grace and mercies to show forth.

The day didn't go smoothly as hoped, the weather was threatening rain. I received a report there was a bad accident on interstate 85 south and my friend must have been talking to himself by now. He looked up and the traffic began to clear and his truck seemed to be riding very low on one side. He checked his mirrors and saw that he had a flat with one of the duel tires on the dump truck. The one good tire beside the flat is very low because of the weight of the load. He drives up the shoulder of the road very slowly, prayerful the tire can carry the load to the next exit.

My friend called me and gave me the blow by blow. He wondered what else could go wrong, rain, traffic accident that shut down the southbound interstate and a rear tire blowout on the dump truck. He drove slowly up the shoulder of the road. When he made it to the exit, everything was closed. This was a Saturday afternoon. I remember praying. I asked the Lord to help me get the flat fixed. Rev. Frank taught us to "Ask God First." He is a jealous God and always wants to be first, no matter the situation, ask the Lord First. There was one repair shop open and getting ready to close. They had one tire, the size that fit my dump truck, I say again, "look at God".

Before they would put the tire on the truck, they needed guaranteed pay. It so happened my driver was short and didn't have a credit card. He called me, I spoke to the shop but she refused my credit card over the telephone line. I heard in the spirit as this warm presence fulfills me almost to tears, "call my deacon". I quickly made the call, he answered. I explained the situation that he needed to take cash forty-five minutes up the road and pay the shop.

When my driver returned home, he explained to me how firm the Lord moved on our deacon. The deacon was about to walk out the door to attend a funeral and the presence of the Holy Spirit moved upon him so strongly his hand was about to open the door, but seemed frozen to the door knob. Then his cellphone rang, I explained the situation and he moved quickly to take the needed funds in cash to get the truck released.

Family, I urge you to tell your story when the Lord had a ram tied to the bush for you. My worse situation, is the Lord's delight to resolve.

TRANSLATION: MARK 3:35 (niv)

God's family is accepting and doesn't exclude anyone. Although Jesus cared for his mother and brothers, he also cared for all those who loved him. Jesus did not show partiality; he allowed everyone the privilege of obeying God and becoming part of his family.

When our lives are in righteous effort in God, we can depend of him with all our cares and needs. My Lord want us to ask him first, He can show us his provision that can fulfilled our needs, whatever it is, my God can supply.

Chapter Nine

PRAYER WORKS

Psalms 6:9 (kjv) The Lord hath heard my supplication; the Lord will receive my prayer.

I have this unique friend. One of the things I learned first, she cared for others and is protective of them. I had a chance encounter with her at a fellowship gathering. I heard her singing. Hearing her, I realized she was an excellent vocalist and a spirit filled daughter of Zion who the Lord equipped to sing His songs in spirit and truth. When she sings, whatever song, it is done with authority and with fire.

After a few years our paths continued to cross. She drove the elderly to their appointments and I had encounters with her getting bread to assist people that had shortages. I was getting bread doing the same thing including going downtown to feed the homeless

This woman of the Lord called and asked for my work uniform because she had a job to do. The school children didn't have a street crossing guard and she was their volunteer to keep them safe on duty in uniform. When she sees young or old men and women folk wavering on the wrong side of life, she speaks boldly to them.

She ministered to a particular young man over a long period of time and thought she would help him secure work in spite of his past life.

We aren't to condemn each other, Jesus taught forgiveness. I remembered she managed to get this young fellow a job trial and soon afterwards he wasn't called back to work. He said to her, "the man didn't call me back to work". She heard in the spirit the Lord saying, tell him he was "monitored." He dropped his head and walked away.

She didn't quit on this young man. She urged him to take advantage of the opportunities when they come. Be willing to take full opportunity for they are few, so make yours count. Next time thank the Lord who transforms us to be more like Him each day.

This woman of the Lord said to me, "Mr. Oscar, the Lord told me to tell you there are two kinds of providers, there are the takers, who gather in and they sleep well at night, but you are a giver, you sleep well every night. The Holy Spirit comes and speaks to you at night in a way he doesn't speak to others". When she said this, I felt the Holy Spirit's presence very strongly almost to tears.

I pray to the Holy Spirit at times, that I trust Him. Out of those private moments, He answers and corrects those issues that causes me to back slide. We are to take on the character of Christ. When I penned this last statement, I felt the presence of the Holy Spirit and this is the essence to the message today; trust the Lord with all and at all times. My children, Jesus Christ is the greatest Love I know and He promised to never leaves us nor will He forsake us.

I raised up very early in the mornings and I came before the Lord with my scriptures, prayers and meditation. I was missing His sweet presence, so I labored before Him and when I least expected late one evening He said, "You Are Back in My Arms Again." I come empty before a full fountain and I'm blessed each day with new mercy and grace, I am forgiven.

Walk each day in the light of the Lord and our chance of stumbling decreases. Our hedge of protection is the light of the Lord.

TRANSLATION: Psalms 6:9 (kjv)

When we pray to our Father which is in heaven and we believe in our heart the Lord hears and answer prayer, then we are to receive it in our heart and be in expectancy and praise the Lord with Thanksgiving from our heart. He is worthy in all things.

Chapter Ten

HE WANTS US WHOLE

James 5:16 (niv) And the prayer offered in faith will make the sick person well; the Lord will raise him up.

My health challenges are getting better, much improved. I must continue to enhance my immune system and my body will stay strong and healthy. I have an appointment with my naturopathic doctor because I continue having high and lows with my energy levels. After a full exam, the doctor says, "you are well however you aren't keeping your regimen with water and exercise I scheduled for you"

I confessed, "You are correct doctor, I have heard in the spirit to drink more water, so I am working towards that improvement."

I tried to feed the doctor a line that I enjoy getting my exercise when working on the lawn, trimming hedges, and painting. That statement, the doctor let it pass by; it was of no consequence. He wanted regular scheduled intaking of fluids and the exercise that he scheduled. With my naturopathic doctor being a man of prayer, I asked the Lord to give him my prescription so it would lineup with what the Lord showed and spoke to me in the spirit.

I shouldn't have launched my own exercise program; the Lord had already given the correct one. I remember in the night watch, I had received a water glass coming to my lips to give me water. I woke and drank some water, said my prayers, went back to bed and slept like a baby. I was sitting in my office chair one day and the Lord unction me to exercise. This is the same prescription the doctor had giving me but I was being inconsistent. The Lord is given me what I prayed for, I must be obedient to do it. Oh Lord I have sinned, I pray now as I write this journal to you, I repent before thee Oh, Lord send your saving grace with mercy, and to others who may have the same problem, Oh Lord bless each of them with favor from on High.

The doctor told me, I'm giving you acupuncture to increase your energy levels. Remember I cleared your negative faults that's pulls you down. You'll need to stay hydrated and exercise is a must, "yes" the one's I demonstrated. When you leave this table, you'll desire to get back to your lawns care. I want my scheduled exercise done daily, after a few days you'll feel strong, then do a little outside but more inside.

My Lord is wonderful. A few nights later He showed me riding my bicycle around my circle driveway. He was saying to do this for my outside exercise until I'm up to par. Thank you, Lord, I'm grateful to have His Love in my life.

I called my friend and we chatted about what the doctor said concerning activating the organs and keeping the lymphatic system flowing. My friend said, "change your water before you do anything else because your body can't fight for itself when the immune system is weak. Choose the right water and the body will hold it longer and you can drink more. It will also do the internal cleansing of impurities from the body. She told me there is a way to improve my water with the new purification filter. This equipment can provide a higher quality of water that we aren't presently experiencing. The Holy Spirit moved very strongly on these words of inspiration and my friend felt His presence as well.

On numerous occasions the Lord indicated that a better drinking water was needed. This word from the Lord didn't come lightly.

The drinking water after it goes through filtration system will be purified and it maintains the minerals.

Family I share this with you, I believe others are experiencing peaks and valleys in their health. The Lord wanted me to share this. After all, He knows all things and He is a

Lord that answers prayers. It takes work and sacrifice to stay healthy to keep the body functioning at a level where we're energized and feeling whole the way the Lord wants us to be.

TRANSLATION: James 5:16 (niv)

The Christian's most powerful resource is communion with God through prayer. The results are often greater than we thought was possible. Prayer is often the last resort, it should be the first act of faith, ask the Holy Spirit for what we stand in need of

Chapter Eleven

HEAR AND OBEY

John 15:8 (niv) This is to my Father's glory, that you bear much fruit, showing yourselves to be my disciples.

When I was younger, I prayed to the Lord. I talked about having a relationship with Him. In the good times I prayed often because I didn't want us to be strangers. If you will, I wanted a friendship with the Lord even though I was younger, healthier, and doing well on my job. In all our lives, the time would come when we will need the Lord. I didn't want to feel guilty and be afraid to call the Lord and ask him to share His saving grace on a sinner like me. I am thankful today, "He calls me friend."

When health, family and work become major issues in our lives, we can bow on our knees and remind the Lord that He promised to hear our prayer and answer us. Our ministry needs are so great that we bow continually with our pastor and prayer teams. God says, "If you trust me, call my name first". My dad says our God is a jealous God. In all my goings I find confidence in seeking His presence and in every way the Lord hears my prayers. He sets me in a quietness called patience while He moves me out of tradition and into a transformative life in Him.

About three weeks ago, I was in prayer and a new member of our prayer team's name came out of my mouth by surprise as I prayed. I had been introduced to her on our prayer team of intercessors. When the Holy Spirit gives me His assignment, I make notes and pray continually.

This morning while meditating after prayer, I heard his voice say, "I will give you a name". This bothered me, and I woke up. I left my prayer quarters and returned to my bedroom and went to sleep. I then heard in my spirit the last name of this person. Before I realized it, I heard the first name and realized it was our new prayer team member. We later found out that we are relatives as well.

When the Holy Spirit is in the plan, all things work together for the good. I talked with her and I invited her to prayer. I welcomed the Holy Spirit in our midst and his presence was awesome.

I declared the word of the Lord to go forth

with authority and power and manifest what the Lord wants to pour out for her and family. I thanked Him for answered prayers. In my spirit I believe there was more to our meeting like this in the spirit. I believe this will be a continuous relationship going forward.

We continued to meet on our prayer line. A couple years later she called and informed me she was coming to Georgia. When she arrived, we got together and talked about our families. We visited a Care Facility and prayed for the residents and went to church together. When we began sharing the family relationships, it turns out that our relationships date back to our mothers' side of the family. Her grand-mother and my mother were sisters.

TRANSLATION: John 15:8 (niv)

When a vine bears "much fruit", God is glorified, for daily he sent the sunshine and rain to make the crops grow, and constantly he nurtured each tiny plant and prepared it to blossom. God is glorified when we develop a right relationship with him and began to "bear much fruit" in their lives.

Chapter Twelve

A MAJESTIC MOVE

Psalm 118:17 (niv) I will not die but live and proclaim what the Lord has done.

I went up town to take care of a promise. I completed my transaction and while there, I purchased a few items for myself and went to check out. There was one person in front of me checking out. I casually observed the cashier while putting my items on the counter. She was not smiling. There perhaps was some discomfort, but she was going through the motions to take care of the customers.

She completed my checkout and I paid her. When she was counting my funds back to me, I saw discomfort in her person. With consideration, I asked "how are you this evening?" She looks and hesitates; as if to say I can't tell this person how I feel.

She replied, I've had a tightness in my chest for a while and I don't feel well. I asked if she had been resting and drinking plenty of water and she said yes. I said "normally I would invite you to use vitamins to support yourself to stay healthy, perhaps you could start a regiment of vitamins, if you are not on anything else."

By now, I was looking closely at her. She had just given me my change and in an instant, the Lord touched me in such a way that I could hardly speak. I heard in my spirit "just heal her,". There were tears in my eyes so I stop talking about the vitamins. I told her, the "Lord wants me to heal you; I am a minister who is called by the Lord to bless your needs, is this alright with you?" She saw the tears beginning to flow down my face, she said "yes". I said, "I do not want to cause a commotion at your checkout, I am going to wave my hand in your presence, then you will be well." I told her, Psalms 91 is her scripture of protection, "read it every night before bedtime, pray to the Lord, he has work for you." What a Majesty Move of the Lord! Later that night I thought to myself, the first choice of vitamin for that young person should have been another vitamin that came to mind. I returned the next day, to complete my original purpose. I looked for her and saw her at her checkout counter. I went into the vitamin section and selected the vitamin and went to her for checkout. She looked at me with a beautiful smile, head high, shoulders squared and I said "hello, you remember me?" She replied with confidence, "yes, I remember you." I paid for the vitamins and handed them to her. I informed her that this will support her to get stronger. She looked at me totally surprised, as I bowed my head and departed.

The Lord says to me, He is an abundant Lord, with a storehouse. If we don't go, He can't share what he has with those who He wants to bless. I want to know when there will be "A Majesty Move," of the Lord. While writing my journal I don't use many scriptures to communicate. In the ministry locations I find myself in, the opportunity is rare. The people are thirsty, hungry and without clothes in many cases. They are filled with doubt, checking us out to see if we are sincere. There are many people who know the word but the Lord is looking for those who are doers of His Word. Our Lord loves every opportunity to show and prove His "Love" for us.

TRANSLATION: Psalm 118:17 (niv)

Let us seek to live to declare the works of God, and to encourage others to serve him and trust him.

Chapter Thirteen

MEEKNESS AN ATTRIBUTE OF CHRIST

II Timothy 2:24-25 (niv) And the Lord's servant must not be quarrelsome but must be kind to everyone, able to teach, not resentful. Opponents must be gently instructed in the hope that God will grant them repentance leading them to a knowledge of the truth.

Today, I visited my hearing doctor to test my hearing. He wanted to see if I had lost hearing since previous test or had it improved. The test results were beneficial and amazingly, my ears had maintained good balance.

Over four years ago, I began to use hearing aids because there were times my clarity of hearing was not balanced. When others were speaking, my hearing was not clear enough to get full understanding. There is a message here that I want the family to glean and adopt. Here is my suggestion for future protection for your hearing benefits.

You must realize that the driving of any large diesel or gas equipment that gives of loud droning noises, when repeated over many years, will affect your hearing. This includes lawn mowers, especially the large units lawn care workers ride. Over a period of time the noise will cause damage to the inner ear. I wore protective head gear and ear plugs when cutting lawns over the many years of my career. That environment still affected my ability to hear clearly. Looking back, I see where I could have done more to reduce the negative affects by always using support devices to reduce the loud and droning noises. Family, I am not trying to be technical. Beware of any loud noises that you encounter over a period of time, it will affect your hearing and your health.

While waiting in the receptionist office for the doctor to call me, I spoke to my spirit. I hoped my healing had taken place by now and I wouldn't need to dread the purchase of new hearing aids. I wanted to complain but the Lord had given me particular guidelines that would enhance the healing of my inner ear by strengthening the affected area. I confess family, I fell of the pathway and didn't maintain the Lord's teaching consistently. I would get back on track and fall short again and so here I am, sitting in the doctor's office with my credit card.

I was escorted into the exam room and at that very moment, this song came into my spirit strongly, "God Will Provide." I was amazed to hear this and wondered what does it mean at this time. In the past, when this song has resonated in my spirit it has blessed me. It gave me hope and assurance that the Lord new my situation and would help me. I was placed in a test booth so I could go through series of sounds with beeps of high and low sounds. The doctor would gather the data and render his findings. The doctor revealed that I needed new hearing aids.

After my test, I ordered new hearing aids. The receptionist showed meekness to the fullness each time I was in her presence. She did the same with others and her kindness always had sincerity of heart. This caught my attention. I stated to the receptionist "you are very kind lending support to us, I want you to know the Lord uses wonderful persons like you that are very caring. The Lord wants you to accept your calling in this ministry to be the blessing he is calling you into." I asked permission to anoint her and she agreed. I called her to do greater works in Christ Jesus' Holy name. This looks to be a chance encounter but the Lord is looking to release soldiers to help build His Kingdom. This was not a chance encounter, it was ordained of God. He needs us be about the Fathers business; it was true then, it is true today.

When, I arrived home I discussed my hearing test results with Prophetess Frankie. I explained that I needed new hearing aids and that the affected area in the inner portion of my ears had not improved. This anointed woman of the Lord said, "I am looking into yours ears, I see through them clearly, whatever was there the Lord has touched you, I declare He has healed yours ears." She continued, "the Lord has touched you, He does not do partially work, it is complete, start praising the Lord, for He deserves all the praise." Prophetess Frankie was in the Holy Ghost, powerfully praising the Lord, over and over and over for what the Lord has done. She stated very strongly with a shout, "the Lord said you are good to go, accept your healing and give thanks unto our Lord and Savior Jesus Christ." I have not worn hearing aids since that encounter with the Lord, "He Will Provide."

TRANSLATION: II Timothy 2:24-25 (niv)

Nothing worse becomes the servant of the Lord Jesus who himself did not strive nor cry, but was a pattern meekness, and mildness, and gentleness to all, then strife and contention. The servant of the Lord must be gentle to all men, and thereby show that he is himself subject to the commanding power of that holy religion which he is employed in preaching.

Those who oppose themselves the truth are to be instructed. Such as oppose themselves are to be instructed in meekness, for our Lord is meek and very lowly, and this agrees well with the character of the servant of the Lord.

Chapter Fourteen

IT IS INVITATIONAL

John 14:13 (kjv) And whatsoever ye shall ask in my name, that will I do, that the Father may be glorified in the Son.

My wife and I received an invitation, to a gala event, celebrating a birthday and releasing the author's new book. We enjoyed the opportunity to take beautiful pictures with her and share in her special moment of success. I confess, the dinner and the location fulfilled all my expectations for an evening with friends, new acquaintances and family.

This is a wonderful and powerful woman of the Lord, and having met her early in her career, she was striding in leaps and bounds in personal studies. Shortly after meeting her, I inquired of her about theology studies and explained my desire to find a qualified school close by. She said, "I can prepare your classes and I would be your facilitator." She had a registered school of theology and her class schedule was convenient for me.

The buffet dinner evening was one to remember. Whatever you can imagine was on the menu. I returned to the buffet line, but I won't disclose the number of times. I returned to my table to eat and another guest was sitting in my chair. I decided to choose another location which separated me from my wife.

I was standing at a table with two occupants

and two chairs unoccupied. "May I join you all please?", "Of course" the young man said. The lady nodded her head, and I quickly learned the lady was his friend. They asked how long I have known the person we were celebrating and I said, "It is a long story, it's been over 18 years."

I was sitting there beginning to eat my dinner but I hardly knew where to start. The couple was very attentive to each other. I thought that this was quite a couple, she was so cordial and respectful. I am amazed when the Lord begins to speak to me through my spirit, I told the lady the Lord had a word for her. I heard in my spirit the lady is quiet and is like and angel, a spiritual being. She is what the Lord likes, someone who is quiet and yet when she speaks you will hear her. I believe I heard, he would bless her with a sound in her voice, that when she speaks normally, the people would hear a sound from the Lord.

While hearing in the spirit she began to cry and she took napkins and dried her eyes. I didn't realize at the time the Holy Spirit had touched her and filled her with himself. He enjoyed doing that because she was quite a soldier. I asked her to keep a journal, from now on. I said "even tonight, because, more than likely I may not remember all that I said". The spirit of the Lord was very high and rewarding while speaking to their needs. I spoke to the friend to let him know, he is the head of his house and the Lord will download into his spirit how to teach his family and raise them up. The lady received instruction to manage the house while he is not available, and they should learn to pray together. While being led by the Holy Spirit, I heard money won't be a problem. The friend quickly said, "I just heard in my spirit 15 or 20 minutes before, the Lord said money won't be a problem." He was visibly shaken, because he had been praying for help on what direction to take. It seems sometimes he is lining up with the Lord's plan and often the Lord is in agreement with him.

I wanted to be clear to the young friend that the Lord will never follow his plan. I said, "the Lord alone is your guide and our total keeper, He will train you to hear him and he wants it all, this means to learn to trust him completely."

They told me of their plan to get funding. I offered a method to assist them in getting the funds and receiving the Lord's plan for their lives. It would benefit them greatly in a few years and the Lord said even less years if they would allow me to assist and work with them on how to manage this particular kind of fund for the future. They seemed very encouraged. The opportunity was before them if they should choose to come forward. "It Is Invitational." My prayer was that they allow the Lord to shape their lives and grow them; for He is the only one who holds the future.

TRANSLATION: John 14:13 (kjv)

Whatever we ask in Christ's name, that shall be for our good, and suitable to our state, he shall give it to us. To ask in Christ's name, is to plead his merit and intercession, and to depend upon that plea. The gift of the Spirit is a fruit of Christ's mediation, bought by his merit, and received by his intercession.

Chapter Fifteen

HEARING HIS VOICE

Psalms 20:2 (niv) May He send you help from the sanctuary and grant you support from Zion.

Family, I am feeling somewhat resolved. I'm here at the Health Institute and after two weeks I'm getting needed rest and health products (green juices) that help greatly in my restoration. Here at the Health Institute we are served breakfast, lunch and dinner. Those who choose to, can eat in the Hall but overall there is a high respect for privacy.

You basically always see me sitting alone. I do enjoy that fact but today two ladies asked if they could join me. I said, "as a matter of fact I was holding a chair for each of you." One of the young ladies was explaining to her friend why she came. The work load at home was over whelming and the workplace was hectic to say the least. She was looking for a place to disappear and recover from the hysteria; to rest and have peace.

I heard a word in the spirit. I didn't want to interfere but the Lord had spoken and it would be safer for me to pass it on than to keep it in. "Excuse me miss, I would like to share a word with your permission". "Who me", she said. "Yes ma'am, the Lord wants you to know, He is "your burden bearer," just leave the matter with Him. You must trust the Lord to answer your prayers".

I believe I saw tears. The Lord of my life

had touched her. I moved into prayer because the fulfilling of the Lord's presence gave me the prayers that would begin to restore her through faith.

I followed the leading of the Holy Spirit and I gave her a "Word," and followed it with "Bread from Heaven," that nourished her. After my prayer, I was silent. I disengaged and became absent, so it seemed. She began telling me her story. I listened with concern and spoke a word that made the difference. "In the future when you pray believe the Lord has heard your prayers, believe nothing less. He is faithful this way, to answer your prayers, they are in His will to do so."

I continued, "Believe this miss lady, there were other tables available even empty ones, but He sent you to my table where He had a word for you, that would give you hope and a chance to restore you in Him and grow your faith to trust Him for it is Him only who saves. I'm an empty vessel until my Lord, our Lord speaks."

The following few days I received numerous invitations to dine, "Can I join you?", "hello sir you can join us if you like." I realized the Lord was moving in our midst and I found other prayer warriors of faith praying mightily for each other. The Lord gave me to prayer and the Holy Spirit filled me with inspirational words that I would speak with great praise to my Lord. If we are asking something of the Lord, it must begin with praise and worship and thanksgiving. He commands us to stand firm that the Word says, He deserves all the praise, glory, and honor. It was my joy to honor the Lord.

When my prayers went out to Him, the Holy Ghost was very present, almost to bringing me to tears while trying to ask of the Lord to meet the needs of the many who was expecting a blessing, healing, job issues and for children who pluck our very last nerve. I submit to you, when the Lord told me, "Oscar, I got the same problems with you", fear struck me and I was definitely afraid.

This Health Institute was intent on total restoration so in addition to eating the good veggies and drinking juices, they had bicycles that were available for us who wanted to ride. I walked out the Hall to get my bike and this gentleman walked along beside me. He was very intent on explaining his health issues and trying to resolve them. His friend joined us and I realized this exercise would be by walking. They were on either side talking to me with serious intent and I could see the expression on their faces that they were concerned about their health.

I looked up the road and another of their friends was waiting for them. When we arrived, he became part of the same issues of health and trying to find the answer. We had walked about a quarter mile and were standing in the middle of the road when it began to happen. My chest was very tight and the fulfilling presence of the Holy Spirit said to my spirit, "if you pray I will bless their health and heal their every need."

This awesome force that surrounded us, I can't explain. The prayer that came forth was like and utterance and the volume of the words was heavy upon me until I prayed all that came into my spirit.

When I came out of the embrace of the Holy Spirit, I looked at the men their hands were clasped there were tears in their eyes and heads bowed. To me this was their humble acceptance they had received the prayers and the Lord had blessed them as He promised. I couldn't walk any further. I was weak and returned to the Hall. At dinner time, the two older gents showed up and were giving testimonies concerning their health status and wanted to start a prayer time to help others.

The Holy Spirit issued a Word to them, they were healed by the hand of the Lord and their assurance was by their testimonies that the Lord has done this. The Lord reached down and touched from His Holy Hill, Mt. Zion, and their lives and we were changed.

The hand of The Lord is with us, let's remember to "Praise the Lord Sincerely" before we start asking. Your honest praise and the love of the Lord, truthfully will touch His heart to hear and act, because His nature is to love His children and meet their needs.

TRANSLATION: Psalms 20:2 (niv)

Nations boast of their great power and might, but David knew that true might of his nations were in worship not weaponry, not firepower but God's power. Only God alone can preserve a nation or an individual, we are to be certain today who we trust.

Chapter Sixteen

YOU ARE NOT ALONE II

Isaiah 54:17 (niv) No weapon forged against you will prevail and you will refute every tongue that accuses you. This is the heritage of the servants of the Lord, and this is their vindication from me.

This Tuesday morning was like many other Tuesday mornings when I drive out to the Decatur Farmers Market and shop for fresh organic veggies. I usually meet my friend and delivery man with the remainder of my fresh grown veggies from his organic farm.

In route home, I received a call from my longtime friend He informed me our best friend had a serious health issue we need to pray. She was rushed to the hospital almost 24 hours ago and haven't spoken or moved since then. My friend said very strongly, "why don't we pray right now" I said, "yes, right now" and I made myself available to pray. I followed instructions and invited The Lord, Our Lord, to join us in this prayer for I alone didn't know the correct words to pray, but through The Holy Spirit we can pray with authority from on High. We would declare the word of the Lord to hold her in His care and heal her body and make her well. "Dear Lord our Lord, we cover her in the blood of Jesus and the healing began by your hand and all the glory is thine

O' Most High, I humble myself before thee at your throne. Amen!"

When my friend and I finished praying, we called Prophetess Frankie, our prayer team leader, to inform the full prayer team to saturate the heavens with our voices as believers and trust Him and Him only to heal our sister in Christ. The astounding part followed immediately when I hung up the call from Prophetess Frankie. I felt a prompting from The Holy Spirit to go to the Medical Center and pray for her.

As we walked into her room at the Medical Center, the husband introduced himself and left her room. The spirit of the Lord was very present and I followed His word to anoint her in the weaken areas. We began to pray and lay hands on her. There was a presence that raised up between us and over her as we prayed.

The Holy Spirit was upon her as we prayed. There was a powerful move of The Lord when she raised her right hand a little and called my friend by name and whispered, "I receive it." He left the room and joined the husband in the waiting room.

I sat with her for a while as the nurse came in and checked her vital signs. I decided to asked a question, "Nurse has there been any movement from our friend since she arrived?" The nurse seemed to give careful thought and said, "she moved her right leg this morning about 10 o'clock."

I said wow, my friend called me about 11:00

am in Georgia and requested me to pray promptly, it was 10:00 in Alabama. I remembered quickly this was about the time, we were praying for her, when I was coming from the farmers market. In the Bible, the centurion can testify of the exact time the Lord did it for him and He is still doing it for them that believe.

My next visit with my friend was at the nursing home a few minutes from the hospital. I arrived with my brother James and our younger brother, Arthur Lee. We were there to thank the Lord for His saving grace and the blessing on her life and the progress she has made. We were celebrating the great works of our Lord Jesus. We gathered around her bed-side and we notice her left leg and side weren't moving. As Arthur Lee began to pray for her, I anointed that area and brother James continued to pray for her and there came such a healing presence of the Lord upon her. When brother James finished, I began to pray. My prayer was about thanking the Lord for what He was doing and I was just so thankful.

When I had finished praying, I whispered to my dear friend, moved your left leg and she moved it. We were in awe of the work of our Lord Jesus Christ and we know that aside from Him we can do nothing.

While penning this testimony, I felt the prompting of the Holy Spirit so strongly that I got from my chair and bowed to my knees to praise Him and thank my Lord for His saving grace.

TRANSLATION: Isaiah 54:17 (niv)

In the coming days, no weapon turned against you shall succeed, and we will have justice against every courtroom lie. These are the blessings that the Lord has laid up for those who trust Him are led by the Holy Spirit. This is the blessing the Lord has given us, so let us walk in them through prayer of supplication and petition.

Chapter Seventeen

WHOSE REPORT WILL YOU BELIEVE

Psalm 118:17 (niv) I shall live not die, but live and declare the works of the Lord.

When we're submitted to the Holy Spirit to serve and be obedient to our assignments, we want to know the mind of Christ. We must learn to obey although we won't always understand why. It becomes very important to follow the leading of the Holy

Spirit.

I was sitting at my desk on Tuesday afternoon and I had an appointment starting in a little while. I decided to pray for the Lord to be present and to continue to fill me with His presence when immediately, at that moment, the Holy Spirit dropped a vision before me of a little girl. She didn't look well. She was standing beside a person and a voice said, "PRAY." I invited the presence of the Holy Spirit to lead me into right prayers for the little child. I wanted to pray the prayers that would heal her every need by the Lord. The Lord brought this to me and issued a command to pray. I prayed all that came into my spirit and I believed she would receive what she stood in need of.

Wednesday morning, twenty hours later, I received a call from our prayer partner. My dear friend had just received a call from his friend; the news was earth shaking. The doctor at the hospital where his daughter lay critically ill, informed him that they have done all they can for his daughter. My dear friend had prayer with the friend for Divine Intervention, trusting the Lord for all he desired and hoped for his child. They asked the Lord to bless, heal and restore. After the prayer with his friend, he called the prayer team. We gathered and we prayed before the Lord with great exaltation for healing and health.

While Prophetess Frankie and Reverend Nancy and the prayer team were praying, I received these powerful scriptures while waiting my turn to pray. My eyes fill with tears, my chest so full I could hardly breath; trying to write down the scriptures I was receiving from our Lord and Savior.

I wrote this as I received it, later I added the translation for a more complete understanding with what this mighty Lord of Lords was saying to his called out ones, his believers.

She Shall Not Die but Live: Psalm 118:17

TRANSLATION: *Let us seek to live to declare the works of God, and to encourage others to serve him and trust in him.*

We Rebuke the Enemy: Isaiah 54:17

TRANSLATION: *Security and final victory are the heritage of each faithful servant of the Lord. The righteousness by which they are justified, and the grace by which they are sanctified, are the gift of God, and the effect of his special love. Let us beseech him to sanctify our souls, and to employ us in his service.*

Whose Report Will You Believe: John 12:38

TRANSLATION: *Sinners are brought to see the reality of Divine things, and to have some knowledge of them. To be converted, and truly turned from sin to Christ, as their Happiness and Portion.*

We Pull Her from The Outer Realm and Established Her Feet:

When I prayed, this virtually was my prayer through The Holy Spirit who leads me in righteous prayers. I believe on the goodness of God and he is the giver of all wonderful and great Gifts. While praying, I believe I heard in my spirit, "We've pulled her from the outer realm and established her feet."

When the Holy Spirit sent me to my knees to pray Tuesday afternoon, I had no idea who I was sending up prayers for. The Holy Spirit gave me the vision Tuesday afternoon, I began to pray through His spirit, so I would pray the right prayer for this child in my vision. Wednesday morning our prayer team assembled and we prayed for revelation knowledge and the blessing from the Lord.

My friend revealed the rest of the story. He informed us about his friend's little daughter whom the doctors had given up. They had provided their best effort to save her but God has the last Word; it belongs to our Savior. This is why we assembled in the name of the Lord and prayed until we heard from heaven. "We pulled her from the outer realm and established her feet."

Family, no matter what it looks like, it may seem hopeless, we are to encourage ourselves. We usher into our prayers all the great works the Lord has manifested into our lives and churches and prayer lines where He demonstrates His saving grace. Each of us have a story to tell, it all speaks to our faith and we have a "Bull Dog Bite," once the Lord give it to us, we won't let go.

We continued to received updates from our prayer partner and was eventually told that the little girl was well.

TRANSLATION: PSALMS 118:17 (niv)

Let us seek to live to declare the works of God, and to encourage others to serve him and trust in.

Chapter Eighteen

THE HOLY GHOST IN MY DREAMS

Psalms 37:5 (niv) Commit your way to the Lord; trust in him and he will do this.

Earlier today, I went out to the farmers market shopping for vegetables and to purchase wheatgrass and buckwheat. These organic products are very good for the body, keeping the blood clean. They are also helpful to the stomach and colon. Afterwards, I went over to see my best friend at the care center. My friend was in good spirits and was getting ready for lunch. Whenever I visit with him, I have him join me in prayer. He always says yes and we call down the glory of God in the rooms and hallways. I then pray for him and I invite the Holy Ghost to come bless all of us and our needs. Whenever I see my best friend, I am so thankful that the Holy Spirit sustained him and blessed his health. When I witness the great works of the Holy Spirit, I am so thankful for the care of the Lord in our lives, and on our health. What and awesome God we serve.

Last night, I was preparing to pray and decided to use my prayer book to choose the right prayer that would help others I pray for. I have a list of family and friends that I keep before the Lord in prayer. I don't launch into prayer. I need to be certain I am in the presence of the Lord who promised if we seek, He will hear us and answer our prayers and heal our needs.

When I opened up the prayer book, it was on the 91st

Psalms. I believe I felt the prompting of the Holy Spirit to use the 91st Psalms in my prayers and there was a blessing late in the night.

When I wrote how I chose the 91st Psalms I believe I was led to it by the Holy Spirit. I was so filled with His presence that I cried like a baby and filled up with His Awesome presence. Now I know the Holy Spirit led me to that chapter and scripture. What blessing. He covers us when we call to Him for help. Knowing that only God can change my situation for the better, I will continue to give all my cares to the Lord and trust Him for my needs.

I was sleeping very sound during the night. Early this morning I heard in my spirit, "I have been waiting for you to Lay Hands on Me." This was a voice, I saw no one. Another voice said, "I Can Do That". The voice sounded like my voice, but I saw no one. When I woke, I felt this warmth spreading over my body and I realized my hands were resting on my right side and the warmth had spread completely over me, this left me feeling well. I desired to be touched and made whole by the Savior, whatever my sins are, they left me feeling undeserving. In my prayers I was ashamed to ask for the Lord's blessing.

Who is this Lord of Lords that comes in the night watch and moves upon the body of an unworthy servant, leaving him feeling well, healed and filled with His presence. The Holy Spirit Has Blessed me. I am prayerfully maintaining my areas of concern with the guidance of the Holy Spirit. I will stop over loading my work assignments and have personal time and quickly go to my knees before the Lord and ask forgiveness.

Family you may encounter at times you will hear me speak of issues with my health while writing my journal. Often my injuries and down times come from disobeying the Lord's instruction to not work long days or stay up late nights with my studies. I reduced but not enough. Then, I'll hit the wall and damage my hands, tissues in my side or some other area. Many times, it stems from my "hard head" my mother would say, but the Lord holds me accountable for my disobedience. Forgiveness is available if we are sincere and pray for forgiveness. The Lord is willing to forgive us of our sins. He is our ever present help and He alone knows all our needs. Sometimes His presence is so close to me, I am overwhelmed. Thank You Lord.

TRANSLATION: Psalms 37:5 (niv)

Commit your way to the Lord; trust in him and he will do it the Lord wants us to give him all our cares and concerns, and trust him to protect and keep his word. He promises to never let the righteousness fall, we must be careful to give the Lord our concerns, and avoid picking them up again. When we pray and give it to the Lord, we must trust him and learn patience.

Chapter Nineteen

DECLARE YOUR FAITH

Luke 7:50 (niv) Jesus, said to the woman, "Your faith has saved you; go in peace.

Early Sunday morning, I was dressed up and attending a local church. At the end of service, I felt encouraged. There were issues touched on by the pastor that gave me clarity and balance. I also believe we are supposed to spiritually prepare ourselves individually to enter into the house of worship to receive those answers we have been in prayer for.

My Mother, Ethel Mae would say we should come to church "prayed up." To be prepared to receive a blessing or be a blessing to someone or for someone and available for the Lord to use you. I can testify, while the Lord had me on assignments, He took care of issues many times for this unworthy servant. I am greatly moved when I can receive nuggets from the message that enhance me. I am strengthened to go forward into my new week knowing my previous week had a good yield from on High. The Master is my Jehovah-Jireh, my provider.

Family, when I am seeking answers from the Lord for those who gave us requests for their needs, I will call on the name of Jesus, a name above every name. I have authority, the exousia is the legal right to use the authority and the might of the Holy Spirit, (Acts 1:8).

I joined my best friend today, we had a few laughs as we talked and prepared for prayer. When I came in and chatted with him he was in good form. He has challenges, so do we all, but has improved tremendously and is peaceful. To the Lord belongs the glory and honor. While there in the center, a ministry group began singing. They had prayer and testimonies as others joined in with their songs and testimonies.

There was a woman of great faith in particular, she gave this powerful testimony declaring she is believing in the Holy Spirit for her healing. She had fallen some time ago and broken her hip and was at this center for rehab. As this service was going on she had the opportunity to tell her testimony. She knew in her heart the Holy Spirit would answer her prayers. It takes a lifetime of experiences with our Lord to have total trust in His Word.

When I heard the claim, I was standing by my close friends and we were engaged in the service. The minister was singing the old-time spiritual songs and we were clapping our hands and patting our feet for the joy of the Lord was upon us. The first time I felt the prompting of the Holy Spirit, I rather ignored it I said under my breath, I'll leave this alone and the Holy Spirit moved me clearly with His presence the second time. When His presence filled me the second time I had to move. I held up my hand and asked if I could pray for all of us. I began and prayed for all. When I arrived to the lady with the declaration that Jesus heals, I prayed and blessed her with healing by the righteous hand of God. I do believe her faith had healed her. There seemed to be a peace that came over her doing my prayer.

Those of us reading this testimony should remember this woman of God had unshakable faith that Jesus the Christ saves. When we go through challenges with family, friends and church members we have a story to tell. Our Lord is the "Great Physician," through Him all things are possible.

The Word of God teaches us to love one another as He has loved us. Family this is why we fellowship in love and have a relationship with each other. I don't know who the Lord will call in the night watch when one of us needs prayer. I hope it would be a friend that I have sat with and shared some things on how good the Lord is to them that believe.

TRANSLATION: Luke 7:50 (niv)

Pharisees believed that only God could forgive sins, so they wondered why this man Jesus was saying that the woman's sins were forgiven. They did not grasp the fact that Jesus was indeed God.

Chapter Twenty

ALWAYS GIVE THANKS

I Chronicles 16:12-13 (niv) Remember the wonders He has done, His miracles, and the judgments He pronounced, (13), you his servants, the descendants of Israel, his chosen ones, the children of Jacob.

On Saturday evening I drove out to the local care center. I try not to stick my nose into situations that seem to be none of my concern. So, it was until one of the great grandmothers spoke to me. I hesitated to say hello and I met a courageous young lady, beaming with a smile, and making a fuss over great-grandmother. It was obviously her pleasure and her delight to be loving on grand mama today.

I was about to walk away and grandmother says, "tell this man to bless your arm." I hadn't noticed that her right arm was shorter than her left. I believe she carried this burden, such as an "outcast" while other children teased her. According to her great grandmother, she had been demonstrating great faith and she understood how to get her arm repaired, once and for all. Great Grandmother said she had been asking various people to pray for the healing of her arm. The faith of this 10 or 12-year-old demonstrates great faith. There was no mentioning of going to doctors, but through prayer it will be taken care of. I speak into your life,

"There Is A Seed in You," it's birthing. Family I am speaking from the spiritual realm in this move of the Lord.

I believe whole heartedly, I was supposed to pass by that evening. Perhaps the young lady had been calling on her heavenly daddy during the night watch and He heard his baby's call and placed the light of the Lord upon her. She did shine bright and He sent the man of God by with a Word to touch her life. If you meet this darling young lady, you would agree she will be walking in the Holy Ghost in the Realm of the spirit saying "Thus says the Lord."

Each time I wrote on the story, the Holy Spirit came upon me so strongly. Filled with His presence I found a safe place to stand. I was in tears and went to my knees with thanksgiving and praises for His awesome works. He knew her heart ached so He healed her wounded spirit and blessed her with the restoration of her arm and hand even as I prayed for her. This was His will to be done and all the glory belong to Christ Jesus The Righteous. I read this today, months later and I am in tears as I added this testimony for us.

On Sunday night, a dear friend was having issues with her eye and asked for prayer concerning her Monday morning eye doctor visit. When she asked for prayer, I received a very strong presence from the Holy Spirit to pray for her. I could sense He would bless her, "She is a woman of God."

She explained that earlier that day in Sunday School, she asked the class to pray for her and she heard my name in her spirit. She decided to be obedient. She called me Sunday night for prayer and expressed the fact that she heard my name in her spirit. I was encouraged because she is His beloved. She's the one who drives the elderly to doctor visits and rises up early morning, to meet the children and assist them crossing the dangerous streets on the way to school. I recognized this prayer was ordained of the Lord. I was careful to pray in the Holy Spirit. The prayer was moving and powerful as I delivered what I heard from on High.

When we had finished praying, the Holy Spirit instructed her to put a warm cloth over her eye; she has a star but would be all right. The next day she went to the doctor and after close examination, he instructed her to take this medication for the infection and put a warm cloth over her eye and she'd be all right. Family with trust and patience, we must continue to be seekers in order to stay in His presence.

If we learn to trust the word of the Lord and learn to be obedient, we will allow Him to manifest Himself in our situation. Always ask the Lord first, then your praises to the Lord, He is worthy to be praised for all the things He has done.

TRANSLATION: I Chronicles 16:12-13 (niv)

True thanksgiving is found remembering what God has done for you and our families notwithstanding the circumstances. With His commandment we are to go and witness to others, the blessing the Holy Spirit has established in our lives, be not ashamed to let your little light shine so others can see your good works. There are many places we can go and give of ourselves and lend support from our resources. If we are truly thankful for the wonders that the Lord has done for us, it is about the great Love, He has for us.

Chapter Twenty One

HE IS IN OUR STORMS

Psalm 91:15 (niv) He will call upon me, and I'll answer him; I will be with him in trouble, I will deliver him and honor him.

I have been in my storms for a while. But, while living in what seemed like uncharted waters, I confess, I have never been alone. I know that my Jesus lives and guides me through every storm. There have been nights that were long and it seemed that daybreak would never come, but even in the long nights, I knew the Holy Spirit was there. Oh Lord you have your way of calming me in the midst of my fears and I am still here today because of you. There is nothing I have done or can do, to earn the love you have blessed me with. I have a Great Father in heaven that I love. I am not ashamed to tell everyone about you; for this is my mission: to serve others and bring you the glory that You deserve.

My prayer is that when you read my testimonies you will feel the presence of the Holy Spirit touch your heart and you will allow the Holy Spirit to lead you by trusting Him to bestow wondrous blessings upon your life. The telephone will ring early in the mornings and someone on the other end will have a word from the Lord. A doctor visit will bring good news, canceling many fears and restoring you to a faithful walk in Christ Jesus.

I remember one day, laying in the emergency hospital bed, having been there all day, praying that the test results would be good. I looked up at the television screen and read, Isaiah 54:17; kjv: "No weapon that is formed against thee shall prosper; and every tongue that shall rise against thee in judgment thou shalt condemn. This the heritage of the servants of the Lord, and the righteousness is of me, saith the Lord." The Holy Spirit calmed me in my fears. He touched my heart with His breath and it drew me to tears. His Word gave me strength and hope to stay in prayer. Even my nurse was named Angel and was as helpful and kind as an Angel.

When I was released from the Hospital and back at home, you wouldn't believe it, I looked out my door and saw two motorcycles come into my driveway. Off came the helmets, it was Angel and the doctor stopping to say hello and see if I was still doing well. Only the Lord can give someone this kind of love and respect for a person that came in through the emergency room.

Right now, I am at my Saturday appointment with the doctor. This visit brings stretching, bending my knees and acupuncture to bring the energy and give me balance. Last night I prayed for the Holy Spirit to come with me and prepare the doctor to do the things on me that are needed.

I asked again this morning that the Holy Spirit would bless the doctor with insight and understanding. The doctor approached my bed and said, "How about prayer before we get started?" I was pleased because we usually do and being a naturopathic doctor, his approach to healing and continued wellness is unique. He introduced me to his assistants. They are prayer warriors and by laying hands on the body through prayer, can help bring healing and restoration.

There was an intervention from me and I had the unction to bless their hands before we began. The experience of their working with my doctor was profound and can only be done through the Holy Spirit. There the Holy Spirit blessed me and I felt restored, strengthen and cleansed. I shared my experience with them so they will know they had participated in a powerful move of the Holy Spirit. I am writing this journal hoping someone else will be empowered and believe the Lord loves us with and Everlasting Love.

TRANSLATION: Psalms 91:15 (niv)

In the Psalms it speaks to our security through the Lord, it teaches us to trust as a believer in the Lord. He may or may not deliver us through all things, but we must trust in Him for the Lord is our full protection in all things.

The Lord is our deliver, so we will hold fast to Him who can do all things. So, we pray that our need for deliverance is in the will of God.

Chapter Twenty Two

BARBERSHOP PRAYERS

Proverb 18:16 (kjv) A man's gift maketh room for him, and brength him before great men.

I had an appointment with my barber on Saturday morning at 09:30 for my haircut. While waiting, I talked with the fueling attendant next door inside at the fuel desk. She tells me she knows my son, Oscar Lee, because he comes there and fuels his buses. When she saw me this morning with my driver getting fuel, she saw my name on my credit card and she knew I was his father.

She admired his respect and kindness toward others and how he fuels the buses for his female drivers. She thought that's admirable, the men she normally sees today weren't very respectful.

I felt the Holy Spirit so I asked had she been praying about something. She said, not really but her sister is dealing with a serious health issue. In His presence I heard health clinic. I suggested an excellent health clinic for her sister after a few words of prayer.

I was finally in the barber's chair getting my hair cut, a couple of Caucasian gentlemen came in for their hair cut and a few minutes later one adult and three children. What caught my eye was the third child being carried by what looked to be a 15 or 16-year-old. The little guy was curled up in his arms and looked to be about 50 pounds and looked very fragile; his arms and legs were very small.

A few minutes later, I felt this warming presence, filling me and it was difficult to breathe. I said under my breath I'm not going to bother with this situation. Then I get a final fulfilling nudge so I said under my breath, I am going to pray. Without praying out loud I prayed for him. As I began to pray within the fulfilling presence came back so strongly I couldn't help but cry and the voice in my spirit said "pray for him, I will bless him". I heard this and felt this presence in my spirit so strongly.

I stopped the barber and told her I needed two minutes of her time. The Holy Spirit was all over me and I was in tears. I then called the young teenager and said "bring me the baby over". I asked the adult male would he mind if I prayed for the child and he said, "go ahead".

The Holy Spirit was so powerful and present that I felt

a healing would take place. When I finished, I reminded them to receive the healing as if it had already been done. After a few minutes passed I heard in my spirit the food the child would need in order to get stronger to carry his fragile body. I gave this to the Uncle to write down. As the barber was finishing up, I told them to put the child down and let him walk. He did this quickly and the little guy took a couple of steps with him holding his arms. I confess, I was so thankful that The Lord had touched this child's life.

The barber was shampooing my hair so my head was all the way back and I couldn't see. When I got up, the little child with his helper had walked across the floor and I marveled at the work of the Lord.

There was a Caucasian middle age man waiting for his hair cut He seemed very curious about what was happening with me and this child. The child came into the barbershop curled up in the young man's arms and now after prayer, he's walking across the floor with a little assistance. The Holy Spirit wasn't finished. I heard the Holy Spirit say, "tell the man he is called out for ministry and to give his life to Christ Jesus." I explained to the gentleman to join a good faith-based church and he would begin to learn more about the Lord. I explained that the pastor will give him guidance toward understanding what it means to be "called into the ministry" and become a disciple for the Lord. I also blessed the two young men but the uncle had gone out. I said to the young man, this isn't the first time you heard that you are called into the ministry to serve the Lord He acknowledged that he heard it before.

For me, this was such a powerful intervention by the Holy Spirit for that family and my barber in her barbershop. I reminded her that months ago, I prayed and blessed the shop and the Lord promised to bless her shop so she had to get herself into place to receive the extra customers. I thank the Lord for blessing the family and child and for reminding another that he is called into ministry to serve the one true and living Lord.

Our take away family, is that we all can be used by the Lord. There are blessings that follow the disciple who says yes to the Lord.

TRANSLATIONS: PROVERB 18:16 (kjv)

Blessed be the Lord, who makes us welcome to come to his throne, without money and without price. May his gifts make room for him in our souls.

Chapter Twenty Three

THE SPIRIT IS HIGH

John 15:16 (kjv) Ye have not chosen me, but I have chosen you, and ordained you, that ye should go and bring forth fruit, and that your fruit should remain: that whatsoever you shall ask of the Father in my name, he may give it you.

I called Prophetess Frankie and we talked for a few minutes. I didn't feel great this morning. She said to call our friend the Reverend, and we will have prayer together. I dialed his number, no answer, so Prophetess

Frankie, shouted "the Holy Spirit is very high this morning", she said "thank you Jesus, hallelujah" and she began to pray. She then asked prayer for her friends' daughter. When she had finished her prayer, she declared all is well.

I prayed for her friend's daughter as well. The Holy Spirit was very engaging. I prayed for the young person, and this statement came into my spirit, "she has a stomach issue, and I sent the cleansing blood of Christ Jesus to bless her needs and I declared the healing in His name, for the Father will be glorified." The love of Christ for his young people is so great. He speaks a word into our spirit because He is just and he wants us whole.

Prophetess Frankie said to try and reach the Reverend because he has a prophecy. I wondered who it was for so I was anxious. I attempted over three times before he answered. He said the timing was just right because he just came into the break room and had a few minutes.

I said, "I called you earlier, the prophetess suggested you should pray for me but since I didn't get you, we prayed for another request. She told me you have a prophesy and I believe the Lord has spoken to his prophet and preacher." He laughed and began to pray for me, and said in his prayer, "whatever you have asked the Lord, it's done, glory to God it is done." I was full of praise to the Lord for he is glorious and full of love. The Lord is the best thing ever happened to me.

His prophecy was given him to speak to their boss for his abusive action towards them. He yells commands and is disrespectful as if it were the old days. The Reverend decided, he had enough. He spoke to his supervisor and told him he was quitting and began to walk out, and the supervisor called him back. At that time, he had a move of the Lord and told the supervisor, "you can't talk to us like this, it's not about race, we are Christians and we won't endure that kind of language and loud talk at us anymore." The supervisor apologized and said he wouldn't act and talk in that manner anymore. This supervisor was standing there crying and was shaken by the presence of the Lord that moved upon them. He demonstrated sincere repentance and his apology was accepted and they forgave him and went back to work.

The next day they came to work and at lunch time, they saw the table filled with food. The supervisor treated all of them with lunch and seemed to have a great relief, having discovered there is a Lord and Savior that helps us to get it right. If we want right living, it comes through faith with a change of heart and we must follow the word of Lord.

TRANSLATION: John 15:16 (kjv)

We all bring honor to God by declaring the dramatic change for good that takes place as a result of being connected to the Vine and thus able to draw upon Him and His power to produce fruit. The disciples should be rich in good works and be striving to produce fruit that endures. God wants the fruit to endure both within themselves by taking on God's character. Mark 16:20 (niv) Then the disciples went out and preached everywhere, and the Lord worked with them and confirmed his word by the signs that accompanied it.

Chapter Twenty Four

AN ATTRIBUTE OF CHRIST IS HEALING

John 15:8 (niv) Herein is my Father glorified, that ye bear much fruit; so, shall ye be my disciples.

It is refreshing to look back on two weeks ago. I walked into my hearing doctor's office to be tested for new hearing aids because the ones from over four years ago had gone bad. I was sitting in the receptionist's office, waiting for the doctor to call me in. While sitting, I was talking to the Lord about my having to buy these expensive items again. I had hoped I would be healed by now, although I didn't follow His guidance to eat certain foods and utilize the other items the Lord gave me to use.

The doctor is very respectful; he came himself and called me into the exam room for my test results. Then, I heard this song in my spirit very strongly, "God Will Provide." I began to look around; why did this song come up now? The songs the Lord sends me always have meaning and I start looking for answers. I began wondering what wrong I have done now. My only hope was that the song was very powerful and sent to encourage me.

The doctor returned and informed me that the results of my tests showed there was no additional hearing loss over the four-year span. So, I ordered new hearing aids to replace the ones that had gone bad.

When I returned home, I called my prayer partner and told her about my doctor's visit. I also told her about the song that came. While I was talking, my prayer partner began to operate in her spiritual gift and began to see into my ears. She explained that she doesn't see anything in my ears except for a little blur. When she said this, I remembered the song the Lord gave me and realized that the song was a confirmation that he was healing my ears.

A few days later I received a call that my hearing aids were ready. They had called me on several occasions telling me my hearing aids were in. I said to myself, I am not looking back, I have been touched by the Lord. I have received this unique blessing and I am thankful. I began to explain to the receptionist about the touch of the Lord and what a blessing to have my hearing again, this is something the Lord done because He wanted to.

While I was explaining to the receptionist what had

transpired, the doctor came to the front, saying good bye to the mother and daughter who was in tremendous need for hearing aids. They had come up from another state where the doctors had denied the daughter hearing aids. I was told by the doctor it is a state law, that a school child must be supplied with hearing aids to attend school classes and be able to participate and increase their learning.

I explained my situation to the doctor and he surprised me by saying, "this is not a problem, if you want, I will keep the hearing aids here for another month if you want me to, or I will send them back and they will send me a credit for you." I further explained that I had not used my previous aids since the move of the Lord to bless my hearing. I said to the doctor, even now the Holy Spirit was very presence in his office and the Lord began to speak to me. What a kind and unselfish doctor he was, that his concern for the client was first and foremost.

I heard "anoint him and I will bless the doctor". I asked permission to anoint him and he said, "yes go ahead". The Lord said he has given the doctor a new level to better meet the needs of his clients. At this time, I was almost in complete utterance trying to gather what all the Lord was attributing to the doctor. The Lord finally said, "I'll give him and office with me, so he has power to get things done". I explained what a tremendous blessing to have and office before the Lord which allows him to hear from heaven.

I suggested to the doctor to call his other offices and some clients, concerning the mother and her young daughter not being able to get hearing aids in her state. I said, "You now have unique powers; the others will hear you and respond." I believe they were turned down, perhaps because they are an African American family. I asked the doctor to please give me a follow-up call with his progress, gaining support for the young lady from out of state they came to Georgia hoping it would work for them.

If we are serious about serving and doing a purposeful work for the Lord, He will guide us into right places. We don't know man's heart. It is delicate so we leave it to the Lord to handle it.

TRANSLATION: (niv) John 15:8

The fire is the fittest place for withered branches; they are good for nothing else. Let us seek to live more simply on the fullness of Christ, and to grow more fruitful in every good word and works, so may our joy in Him and in his salvation be full.

Chapter Twenty Five

IT WAS EARLY

Psalms 30: 1-4 (nlt) I will exalt you, Lord, for you rescued me. You refused to let my enemies' triumph over me. O Lord my God, I cried to you for help, and you restored my health. You brought me up from the grave, O Lord. You kept me from falling into the pit of death. Sing to the Lord, all your godly ones! Praise his holy name. For his anger lasts only a moment, but his favor lasts a lifetime.

I couldn't sleep. I was in bed at 12:10 am and I woke at 02:30 am. I tossed and turned but I couldn't find sleep. I came to my office and prayer quarters and began to read. Afterwards, I had prayer and for the first time, I wrapped myself in my prayer Shawl while doing my prayer. I was praying on my knees with my arms on my chair looking out my east window. I was in deep prayer with my eyes closed and I began to get this oil fragrance radiating up to my nostrils. I couldn't imagine where it was coming from. I smelled my arms and I had not used any anointing oil, even if I had, I do not have any that smelled like this fragrance. It had a light odor of musk, but its presence was powerful.

I didn't realize it at first but I had begun to shed tears. In my spirit I realized I was in the presence of High Authority. My arms fell from the chair, and I bowed to the floor in fear and humbleness that I was in the presence of the Lord.

When I had finished my prayer, I went back to bed and shortly afterwards, I heard four words and I wrote them down the way I heard them.

1.) REFRESH; (a.) To make fresh or fresher, as by cooling; to restore strength, spirit. (b.) To revive, strengthen, or the like, by or as by renewing supplies; replenish; as, to refresh one's memory. c.) To freshen up, as by cleaning; renovate d.) To become fresh again; revive. e.) To give supply, or take refreshment.

2.) RENEW, (renu) v a.) To make new again; to restore to freshness or vigor; also, to gain again as new; as, to renew one's strength. b.) To make new spiritually; to regenerate. c.) To re-establish; rebuild; revive. d.) To repeat; go over again. e.) To recommence; resume; as to renew an attack. f.) To replace; also, to restore to fullness; as, to renew water in a tank. g.) To grant or obtain an extension of; as, to renew a note. - v.a.) a.) To become new, or as new. b.) To begin again; resume. c.) To make a renewal as of a lease. -

renewable, adj.

Syn. Renew, restore, refresh, renovate, rejuvenate means to make new or like new. Renew implies unusually a replacing of that which is decayed, disintegrated, or like; restore, a return to an original state after depletion, illness, etc.; refresh, a supplying of something that restores lost strength, animation, etc; renovate, a renewal or refreshing of, usually, a material thing; rejuvenate, a restoration of youth vigor, appearance, powers, etc.

3.) Restore' (re-stor'; v., [OF. restorer, fr.(in comp.) to place, fix.] a.) To give back; to return. b.) To re-established; to put back; into existence or use, as harmony among foes. c.) To bring or put back; to put (a person) again in possession; as, to restore a king to the throne. d.) To bring back to, or put back into, former or original state; to repair; renew; specif.: a.) To reconstruct. b.) To reinstate in a former in a favor, position, office, etc. c.) To bring back into a healthy state. d.) To renovate, as a painting. e.) Arch.

Jeremiah 30: 17; For I will restore health unto thee, and I will heal thee of thy wounds, saith the Lord; because they called thee and Outcast, saying This is Zion, whom no man seeketh after.

To repair and alter (building) into nearly or quite the original form. --<u>In this the Holy Spirit brought me to tears.</u> -- restorer--

4.) BUILD: building, Archaic past & past part. builded. [AS. byldan to build, bold house,] a.) To unite materials in order to fabricate or make; erect; construct.

b.) To create or produce gradually as a result of effort, system, etc.; as to build up a practice. c.) To establish; found; as; to build as on a foundation; Form or mode of construction; general figure; make—builder.

TRANSLATION: (NLT) PSALMS 30:1-4 (nlt)

The great things the Lord has done for us, both by his providence and by his grace, bind us in gratitude to do all we can to advance his kingdom among men, though the most we can do but little. God's saints in heaven sing to him; why should not those on earth do the same? Not one of all God' perfections carries in it more terror to the wicked, or more comfort to the godly, than his holiness.

Chapter Twenty Six

"URGENT CARE" CALL OUR LORD

Psalms 107:20 (kjv) He sent his word, and healed them, and delivered them from their destruction.

My longtime friend had promised to help me clear some trees on his next days off. We were working the second day and by accident, he received a cut. We went to the Health Center for attention. They cleaned his wound, put stitches in and sent us home. They questioned his pain and he said, "there is none."

After the procedure, we drove home. I asked about the pain level and he said there was none. I realized that I had already began to pray for the Lord to take care of my friend because he came to assist me on his day off. From the time he had the injury and after medical attention was given, my friend said he had no pain. I believe the Lord had interceded and taken care of him. Over the years my friend always had his very own place with the Lord. The Lord protected him on his job and renewed his health over the years. This is something the Lord wanted to do for my friend. The painlessness was instant and taken up by the Lord, blessing my friend so. I am reminded that our Lord looks at the heart. His love is so fulfilling.

The doctor instructed my friend to return in eight days and he would remove his stitches. He returned, the doctor asked, how was your pain, my friend tells the doctor that he didn't have any pain. His doctor gave him a curious look and accepted his statement. Our

Lord was at work. When the Lord moves, it is evident and is good for witnessing. What the Lord has done for my friend, He will do for you if we learn to trust Him.

My desire in this narrative, I want the message to be received in its fullness for those who need to learn to trust the Lord. Take a look into your lives and see how the Lord has manifested himself by healing us and bringing families together. When the Lord manifests himself in our lives, He is growing us and drawing us closer to him so we can trust our Lord Jesus Christ. When we begin to let the Lord be our first choice in our situations, He can increase us.

I went with my friend to have his stitches removed. While waiting, I was eating cookies and a young man was holding his young baby. I shared my cookies with them. I heard the baby groaning in discomfort and the man said the baby was sick, but her mother is very sick. When that was said I felt the presence of the Holy Spirit. I thought I should pray for them. I asked the young man if I could pray for them, he said, "yes, thank you." I thought to pray over the father and it would bless the baby and wife. The presence of the Lord was very strong, to say the least.

I discussed this spiritual undertaking with Prophetess Frankie, and she began to speak in the spirit, that the prayer was meant for the mother and she received the blessing and would improve.

TRANSLATION: Psalms 107:20 (kjv)

All Christ's miraculous cures were emblems off his healing diseases of the soul. It is also applied to the spiritual cures which the Spirit of grace works.

He sends His Word, and heals souls; convinces, converts them, makes them holy, and all by His word.

ABOUT THE AUTHOR

Oscar Dixon

I was born in Roba, Alabama, August 29, 1942 to Ethel and Rev. Frank D. Dixon, he was a pastor in the Alabama A. M. E. Zion Church Conference. I gave my life to Christ at a very early age, about ten or eleven years old, and were baptized and joined The County Line A. M. E. Zion Church, under the pastorate of Reverend Robert Day.

Through prayer and fasting, I learned, I was called into the ministry at the tender age of fourteen by our Lord, Jesus Christ. As I grew up, I had many encounters from my youth to adulthood, my parents, explained these events, and finally they said we were peculiar children.

I am married, to Mrs. Gloria Allen Dixon, for over 54 years with two children, Oscar Lee and Melinda Rae Dixon Chapman. We are grandparents to Oscar Najee and Natosha Dixon Porter, who gives us two great grands, Imani and Zechariah. When the Lord called me this time, he got my attention, I had retired from my job, and was in my late fifties. I had built houses and was renovating properties. Doing this time, I became very sick and, I didn't feel so deserving, but the Lord turned my fears into joy. My church family new of my struggles with my health and they prayed without ceasing, I remember my pastor saying to me brother Oscar we are praying for you.

While working on my property, the Lord called my name, He asked me "Will You Serve Me," I said yes, and I have not looked back, but sought every opportunity to prepare myself to be able to serve. I took my theology studies from Beacon University, Columbus, Georgia, I achieved my Associate Degree, and bachelor's degree of Theology. From the Christian Life Studies of Theology, I achieved my master's degree of Theology in 2013, and my Master of Sacred Studies in May of 2019. I have two years local preacher and one year traveling minister in The African Methodist Episcopal Zion Church.

In 2005, I was invited to come on a mission trip into downtown Atlanta, I am still here working in 2017. I volunteered to work in two health and rehabilitation facility, I began in 2007 and 2008. There is a take away in this spiritual focus, remember when you pray, believe what you have prayed for, and receive it has thought it has already manifested itself, because The Lord answers prayers.

www.ingramcontent.com/pod-product-compliance
Lightning Source LLC
Chambersburg PA
CBHW021157160426
43194CB00007B/779